FISHING SKILLS

Roach Fishing

Tony Whieldon

Introduction by Dave Coster

WARD LOCK LIMITED · LONDON

© Ward Lock Limited 1988

First published in Great Britain in 1988
by Ward Lock Limited, 8 Clifford Street
London W1X 1RB, an Egmont Company.

Printed and bound in Italy by New Interlitho, Milan

British Library Cataloguing in Publication Data

Whieldon, Tony
  Roach fishing.
  1. Roach. Angling – Manuals
  I. Title II. Series
  799.1′752

  ISBN 0-7063-6693-X

Contents

Introduction

A fish that is undoubtedly the most fished-for species in this country, certainly the most prolific, arguably the most adaptable and possibly the most elusive when it reaches specimen proportions: we are, of course, talking about the roach!

Roach can be found in a variety of waters from the tiniest stream to the largest river. They also live in lakes, vast meres and reservoirs – filtering down to small, sometimes even semi-polluted farm ponds. Then there are the fens and drains irrigating our flatlands, and the vast network of canals which criss-cross the country. If a water holds fishlife, it is a fair bet the roach will not be far away.

Small roach are often easy to catch, and in contained waters like park ponds and short sections of canal they multiply very quickly, often becoming stunted in the 2-4oz bracket. This is not a bad thing from the young schoolboy's or novice angler's point of view. These teeming shoals will mop up most recognized small fish baits thrown at them, so there is plenty of action to be had while honing one's fishing skills.

Such is the fascination of roach fishing, however, that it is rarely very long before the angler is seduced into the finer arts of trying to tempt larger specimens of this ever popular fish. This leads on to specialized techniques like hemp fishing with the pole, waggler fishing at distance with maggots or casters, or trotting flowing waters with the stickfloat, avon or balsa. Then there is the more leisurely approach: laying-on near the rod tip with bigger baits like breadflake, sweetcorn,

worms or cheese. Most forms of legering will also find those better-sized roach. This book covers all these methods, and the individual will soon no doubt adapt to his own favourite styles as he gains experience with each.

The diversity of roach fishing is such that you could choose to fish a heavily coloured lake or canal where the roach might appear very pale and silvery with just a tinge of red in their almost bleached-looking fins. Or you can just as easily opt for a clear running river like the Hampshire Avon or Dorset Stour where these fish will be in mint condition, showing off brilliant orange/red fins and a lovely fresh sheen of blue down their backs. Then again, on larger lakes you will probably find the bigger roach tend towards an olive-green appearance, when viewed from above, and their flanks are much more bronzed than those of their river cousins. The roach somewhat mirrors its environment.

The current record roach is 4lb 1oz and came from a gravel pit fishery. But in setting your sights on a good fish, it should first be understood that the 4-pounder on our record lists was a very exceptional fish, perhaps a one-off, never to be repeated. Generally in angling circles 2lb is the magic weight which signifies whether or not you have caught a real specimen, although this, too, can be misleading. A fish of 1lb taken from certain hard-fished, gin-clear canal venues, is certainly a good catch, but it does not represent a very big fish from a renowned roach river like the Kennet. To put it plainly, a fish of 1lb *is* a good size, a 1lb 8oz roach is a most worthy achievement, and a 2-pounder is many angler's lifetime ambition!

Two-pound fish are still surprisingly common in our top roach rivers, tending to fall to rod and line in late autumn or winter, when the first frosts have reduced the weed growth. Otherwise, if you want an outsized fish, your best bet is to concentrate on gravel pits or reservoirs. But be warned: these are not easy fisheries, and although the fish may be big, they are often few and far between. However, don't despair! A big roach can still turn up virtually anywhere. Even on small venues where most of the fish seem to have come from the same mould, a really big specimen can and often does turn up out of the blue.

To be successful at roach fishing you will first need to learn where to find the fish and, as you will discover later in this book, each type of water has its own peculiar traits in this department. Then you must learn the art of feeding to attract the fish to your hookbait. This can entail various methods, from using quite solid groundbait in flowing water, to very gentle loose-feeding in lesser flows or stillwater.

Tackle is just as important. Stiff-actioned rods and heavy lines have no place in the roach angler's armoury. Finesse is the name of the game, in some cases scaling down to fragile 1lb lines and fine-wire 20 or 22 hooks to try and outwit wily clear-water fish.

End-tackle needs to be properly balanced, too. Big roach will not be fooled by hookbaits that behave erratically. Presentation has to be spot-on, and this can involve fishing at a variety of depths, much depending on the time of year. Roach can feed just as avidly on the surface when water temperatures are high as in mid-water; regular feeding will often pull the fish up to these levels if there is a good-sized shoal in the swim. But the experienced angler may well learn how to keep the fish on, or near to, the bottom by modifying his feeding techniques in order to get more positive bites.

The magic of roach fishing has much to do with the large selection of baits and tackle that can be used. There is a method to suit most anglers' tastes, whether novice, pleasure angler, clubman, specimen hunter or matchman. Tony Whieldon has really covered the whole spectrum of roach fishing with his graphic artwork, which illustrates in a way words and photographs cannot. Every page is brimming with valuable tips and wrinkles which will help you to catch fish. Recommended tackle is up to date and easily obtainable, and the rigs described are easy to follow; again, thanks to Tony's unique expertise with brush and pen.

Dave Coster,
London.

October 1987

Roach

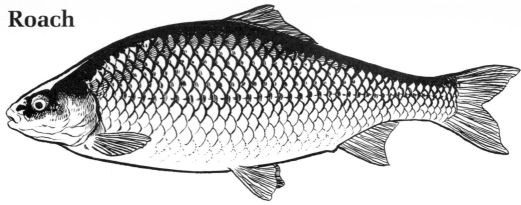

Roach are found in profusion throughout most of Europe, therefore it is not surprising that they have so many devotees. Roach are attractive fish— the iris of the eye is red, the fins orange and red, and the large scales shine silver, deepening to bronze as size increases. The colour of the back varies from blue to olive green.

The largest roach ever taken on rod and line in Britain weighed 4lb·1oz (1·80kg). It was caught in 1975 by Richard Jones, from a gravel pit in Nottinghamshire.

Erroneous identification is common as roach are similar to rudd, to the uneducated eye. The points shown below will usually be sufficient to establish true identity.

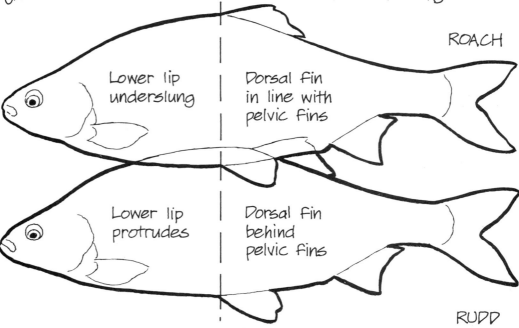

ROACH

Lower lip underslung

Dorsal fin in line with pelvic fins

Lower lip protrudes

Dorsal fin behind pelvic fins

RUDD

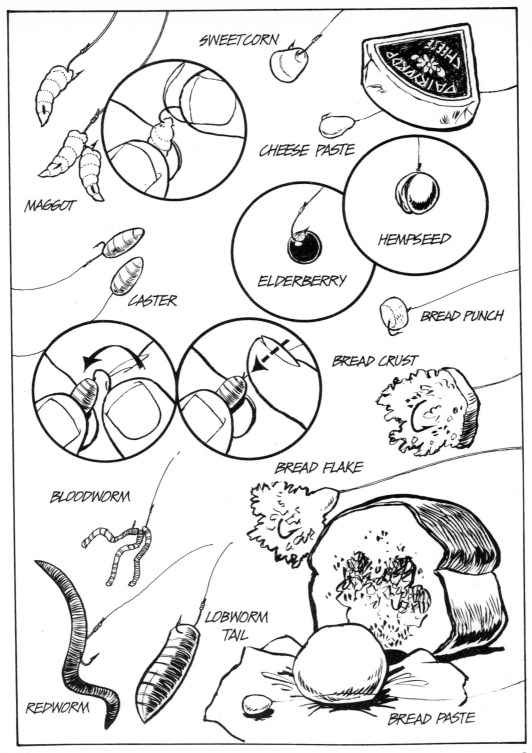

SWEETCORN

CHEESE PASTE

MAGGOT

HEMPSEED

CASTER

ELDERBERRY

BREAD PUNCH

BREAD CRUST

BREAD FLAKE

BLOODWORM

LOBWORM TAIL

REDWORM

BREAD PASTE

9

Float fishing tackle for roach

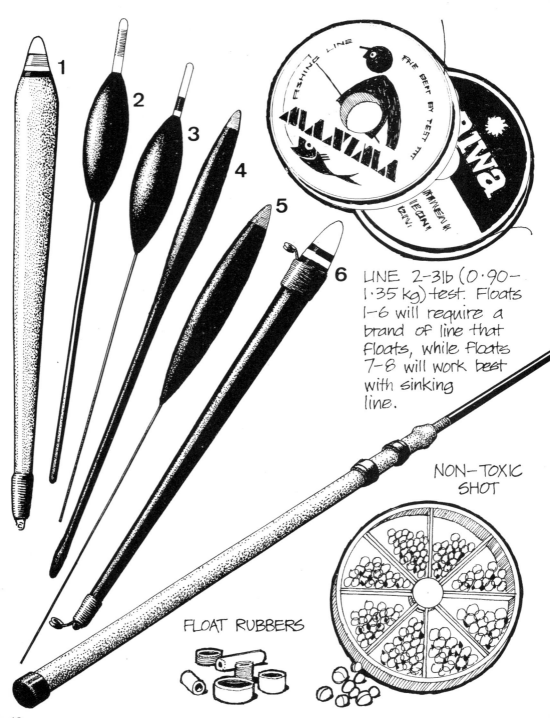

LINE 2-3lb (0·90–1·35 kg) test. Floats 1–6 will require a brand of line that floats, while floats 7–8 will work best with sinking line.

NON-TOXIC SHOT

FLOAT RUBBERS

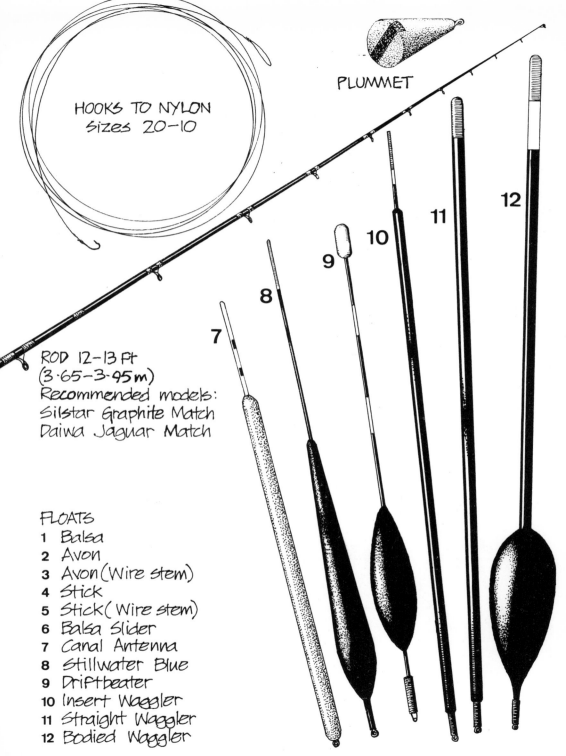

HOOKS TO NYLON
sizes 20-10

PLUMMET

ROD 12-13 Ft
(3·65-3·95m)
Recommended models:
Silstar Graphite Match
Daiwa Jaguar Match

FLOATS
1 Balsa
2 Avon
3 Avon (Wire stem)
4 Stick
5 Stick (Wire stem)
6 Balsa Slider
7 Canal Antenna
8 Stillwater Blue
9 Driftbeater
10 Insert Waggler
11 Straight Waggler
12 Bodied Waggler

Groundbait

Groundbait consists of a base of brown or white crumb, which is best bought in bulk. Store in a dry place above ground level.

Mixing 1

Pour about 3pts(1·704 Ltr) of cold water into a 2½ gal (11·36 Ltr) plastic bucket.

2

Add an amount of crumb to the water and mix, with the hands.

3

If the resulting mix tends to be too dry add a little more water and knead with the hands once more. The ideal mix is one that allows the crumb to be moulded into a ball.

Consistency

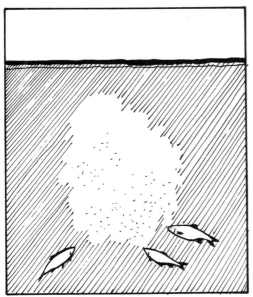

A wettish consistency will result in the ball disintegrating as it hits the water, producing a cloud effect which is effective at close range when smaller roach are the quarry. To avoid disturbing the swim, use balls no larger than golf-ball size.

A more solid consistency is best for transporting the bait, intact, to the bottom where it will slowly disintegrate.

Additives

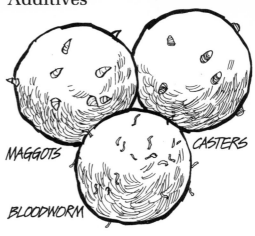

MAGGOTS   CASTERS

BLOODWORM

In recent years the popularity of continental additives has continued to increase and all good tackle stockists now have a large variety of aromatic essences.

Stillwater float fishing

The best time to pursue stillwater roach is during the summer and autumn, the latter season being the better of the two. Roach in ponds and smaller lakes, where marginal weed growth occurs, are easy to locate, and it is in this scenario that most beginners have their first encounter with the species.

There is one very important item of equipment which is often overlooked by the tyro. This is the plummet, with which to ascertain the exact depth of the swim about to be fished.

Finding the depth

Estimate the depth and fix the float in position. Hook a plummet to the end of the line by passing the hook through the eye at the top and inserting it into the cork at the base. Using a pendulum swing, lob the plummet into the area to be fished.

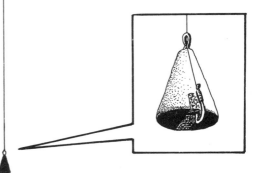

FLOAT SET TOO LOW
(ADJUST)

FLOAT SET TOO HIGH
(ADJUST)

CORRECT
DEPTH

The antenna-type float is best suited to fishing at close range on ponds and canals when conditions are perfect, with no wind or surface drift.

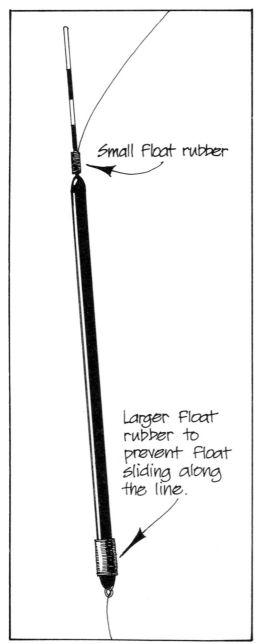

Small float rubber

Larger float rubber to prevent float sliding along the line.

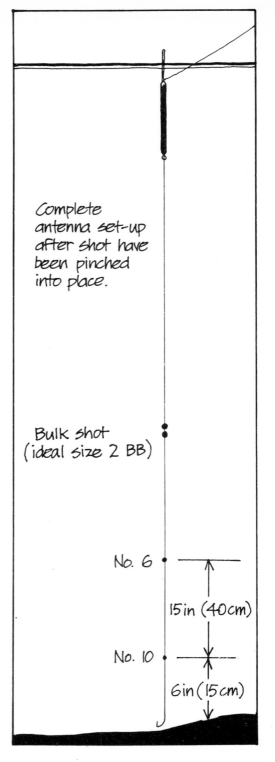

Complete antenna set-up after shot have been pinched into place.

Bulk shot (ideal size 2 BB)

No. 6

15in (40cm)

No. 10

6in (15cm)

One or two small balls of brown-breadcrumb mix laced with maggots, soft enough to break up and form a cloud in the water, will draw the fish into the swim.

Golf-ball sized offerings will produce an adequate effect without spooking the fish. Subsequent loose feeding with a few maggots, from time to time, will hold the fish in the area.

Bites are usually signalled by the antenna rising as the fish lifts the bait and bottom shot, and should be struck quickly.

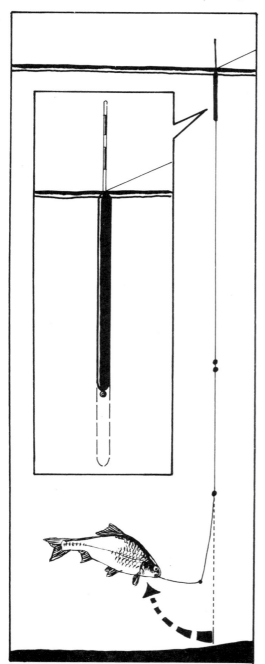

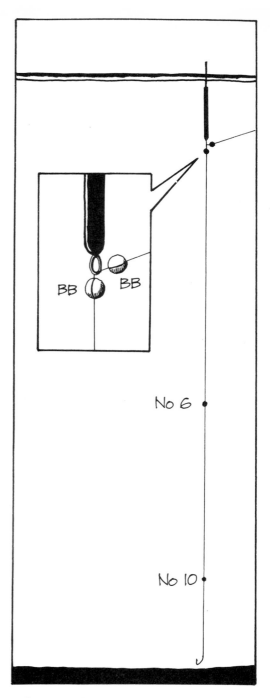

BB   BB

No 6

No 10

Alternative method for attaching the antenna float using two split shot.

Another excellent float for close-in fishing is the Peter Drennan Stillwater Blue. This float can be employed using the same shotting pattern as the bottom-attached antenna.

Alternative set-up for slight surface drift — the float is moved up the line to allow the bottom shot to rest just on the bottom.

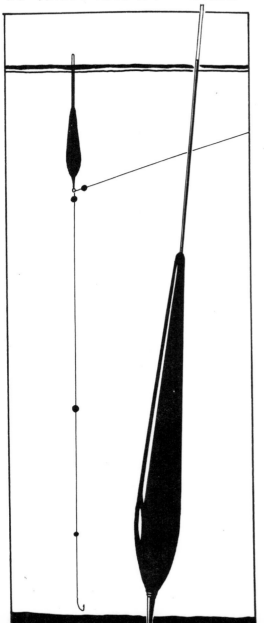

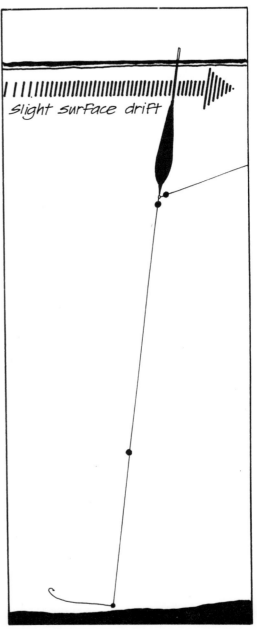

Slight surface drift

When a bottom-attached float is being used the line must be submerged between the rod tip and the float, even for close-in fishing.

(A) Cast beyond feeding area.

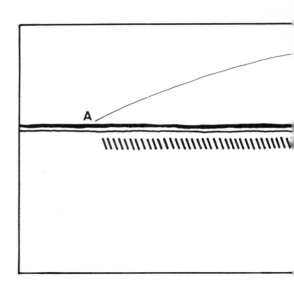

(B) Lower rod tip beneath the surface and retrieve line.

(C) Stop retrieve to allow shot and bait to sink into feeding area.

The following sequence shows the typical behaviour of a float as the terminal tackle sinks into the feeding area.

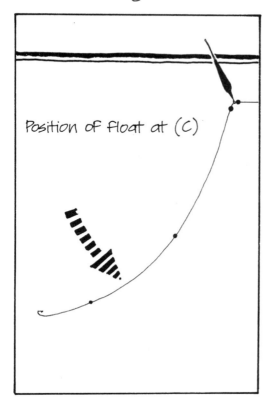

Position of float at (C)

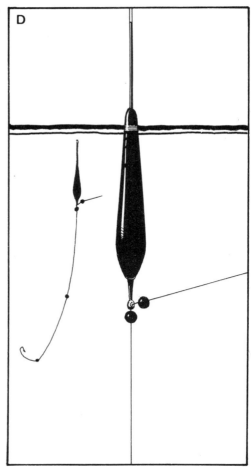

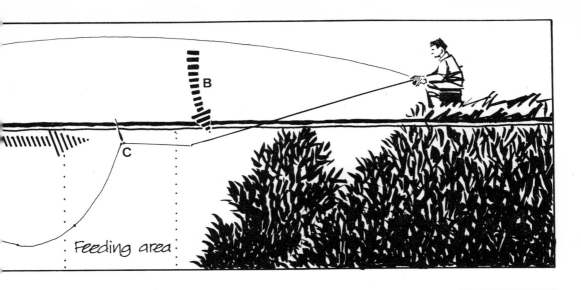

Feeding area

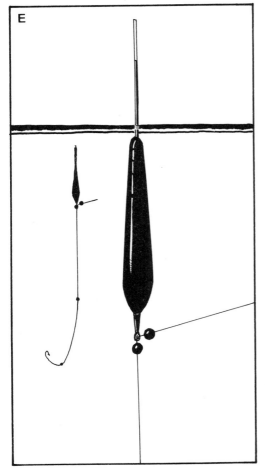

E

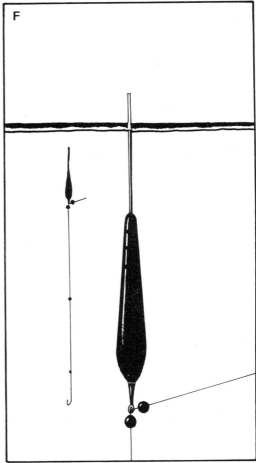

F

Roach will often rise well up from the bottom to intercept sinking loose feed items and hook-bait. Therefore, any unnatural behaviour by the float during this period should be regarded as a bite, and struck immediately.

Fishing on-the-drop

Examples

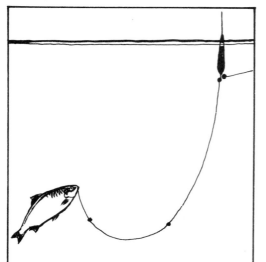

Float remains in position 'D' longer than usual as fish intercepts bait, preventing both bottom shots registering.

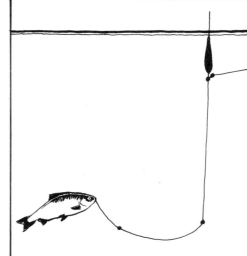

Float remains in position 'E' longer than usual as fish intercepts bait, preventing bottom shot registering.

Peacock quills in different lengths are always a useful addition to the roach fisher's armoury.

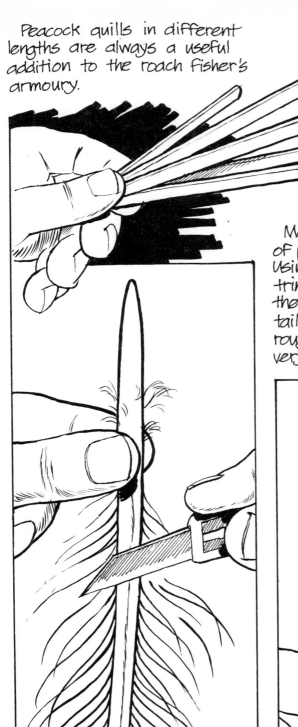

Making up your own lengths of peacock quills is simple. Using a sharp craft knife, trim the fibres away from the thick end of a peacock tail feather, then remove any rough or furry areas with very fine sandpaper.

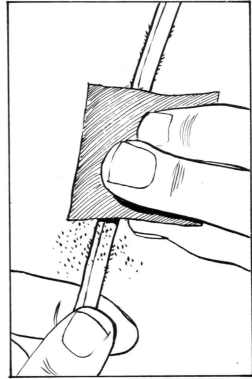

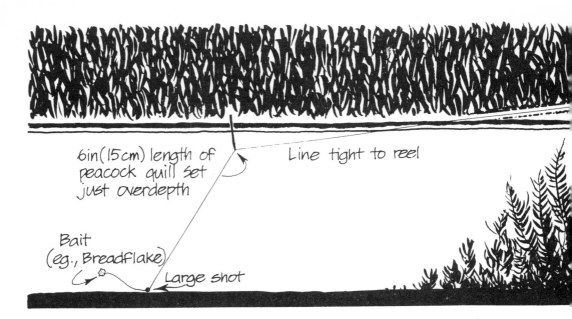

6in(15cm) length of peacock quill set just overdepth

Line tight to reel

Bait (eg., Breadflake)

Large shot

The lift method

Peacock quill is ideally suited for use with the lift method, which is often used for tench, but is equally effective for large roach in medium—depth water. The rig is simple and sensitive, presenting the bait exactly where big roach want it— on the bottom.

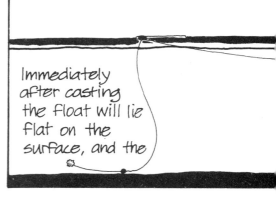

Immediately after casting the float will lie flat on the surface, and the

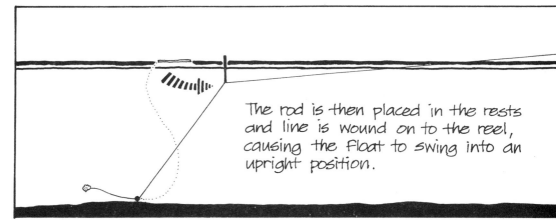

The rod is then placed in the rests and line is wound on to the reel, causing the float to swing into an upright position.

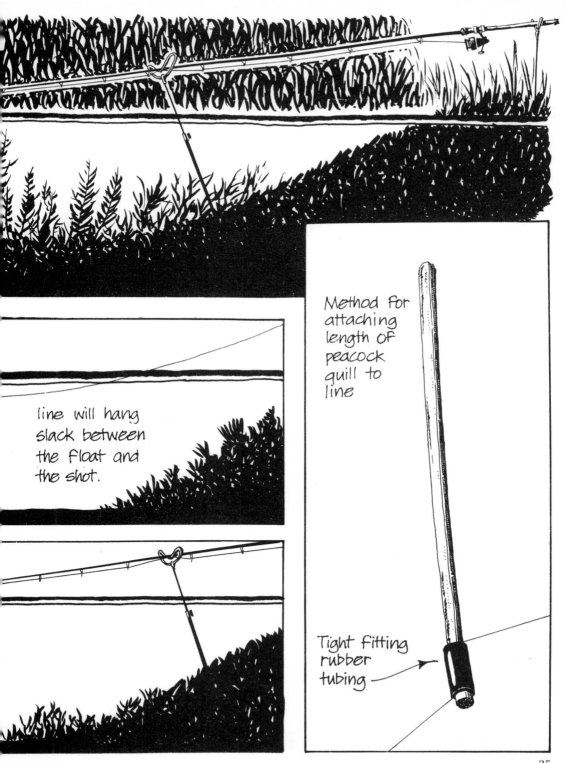

line will hang slack between the float and the shot.

Method for attaching length of peacock quill to line

Tight fitting rubber tubing

Two ways of resting the rod while waiting for a lift bite.

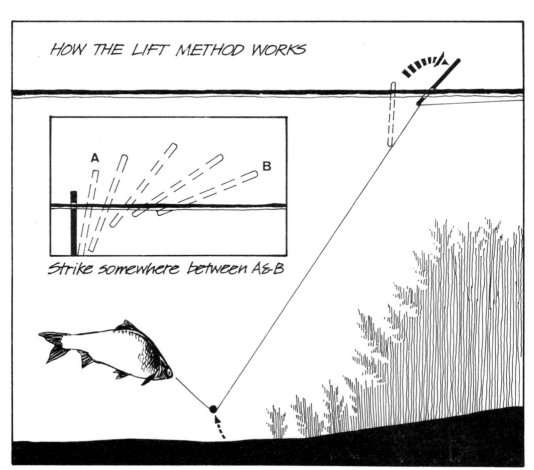

HOW THE LIFT METHOD WORKS

Strike somewhere between A&B

Float leger

This was the method used by Bill Penney to catch a 3lb 14oz (1.77kg) roach from Lambeth Reservoir, which held the British record from 1938 until 1975.

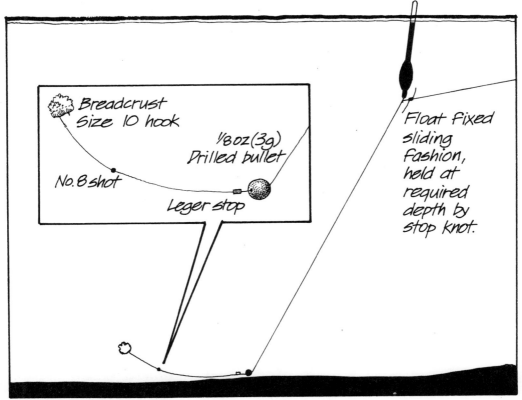

Breadcrust
Size 10 hook

⅛oz(3g)
Drilled bullet

No. 8 shot

Leger stop

Float fixed sliding fashion, held at required depth by stop knot.

Longer-range stillwater floats

Roach are not always close in and casts of some three or four rod lengths may have to be made in order to place the bait in the area of the shoal. This approach will necessitate the use of a more substantial float, both to carry the shot needed for longer casting and also to overcome the drag problem which arises in all waters exposed to wind and surface drift.

The floats shown, sarkandas reed-tipped and straight peacock wagglers, about 10 or 11 in (25 or 27cm) in length, will usually cope with slight to moderate surface drift and wind.

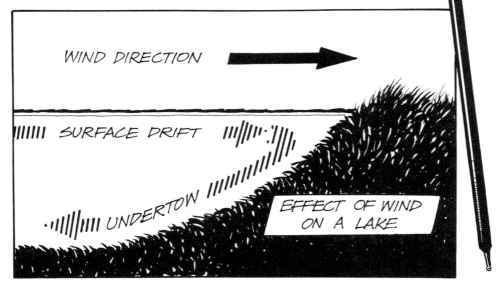

WIND DIRECTION

SURFACE DRIFT

UNDERTOW

EFFECT OF WIND ON A LAKE

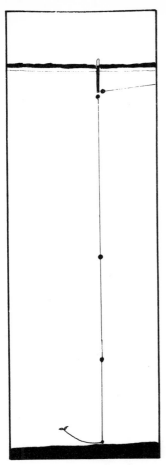

Standard shotting   Overcomes slight drag   Overcomes bad drag

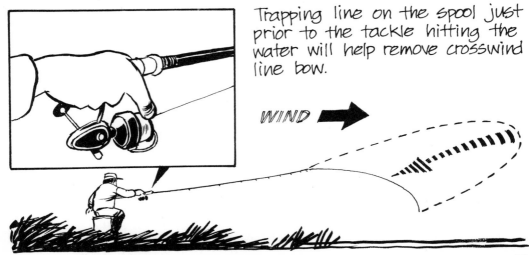

Trapping line on the spool just prior to the tackle hitting the water will help remove crosswind line bow.

WIND →

Even when the line has been sunk after the cast the flow may still create a slight bow.

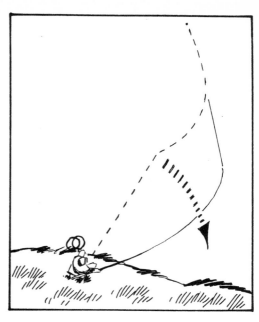

STRIKES SHOULD ALWAYS BE MADE IN THE DIRECTION OF THE BOW.

More serious wind problems can be tackled with the windbeater float which gives excellent lift-bite signals.

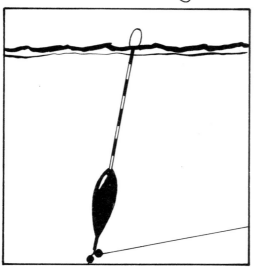

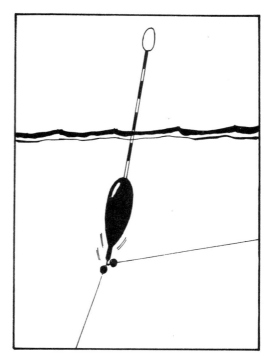

Hooks

RED MICROBARB

DRENNAN ULTRA-FINE POLE HOOK

DRENNAN CARBON CASTER

DRENNAN MATCH

BARBLESS KAMATSU

RED KAMATSU

6

8

10

12

14

16

18

20

Spade-end hooks already tied to nylon are ideal for float fishing. It is, however, a wise precaution to check every knot before use as some have a nasty tendency to come adrift at the wrong moment. Some anglers play safe and tie on their own.

Eyed hooks are an alternative, and here it is wise to check the eye to ensure that it has been properly formed.

BAIT	HOOK SIZE
BLOODWORM · MAGGOT	20
MAGGOT · CASTER · BREADPUNCH	18
CASTER · MAGGOT · HEMP · ELDERBERRY	16
REDWORM · MAGGOT · ELDERBERRY	14
BREAD PASTE · CHEESE · REDWORM · SWEETCORN	12
LOBWORM TAIL · BREAD CRUST · BREAD FLAKE	10
LOBWORM TAIL · BREAD FLAKE · BREAD CRUST	8

Hooklengths will range from 1lb (0·45kg) to 2½ lb (1·15 kg) breaking strain.

Hooklengths can be attached to the main line by using the double loop method.

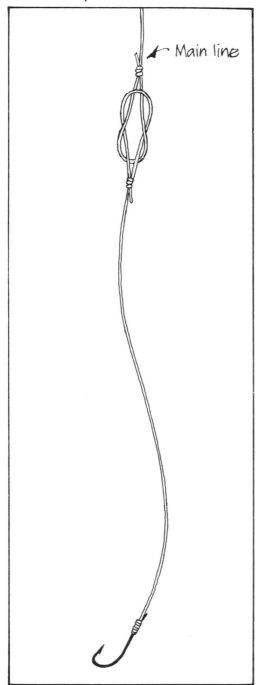

Main line

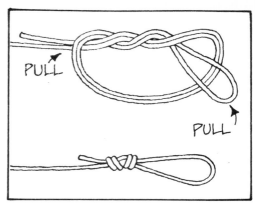

PULL

PULL

Method for tying loop knot.

Spade-end hooks can also be bought loose and whipped to a hooklength as shown below.

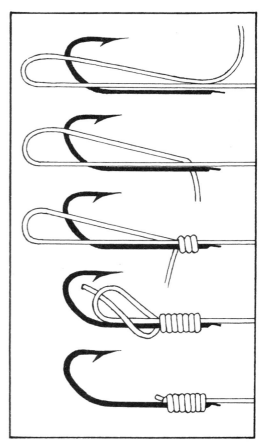

Knots

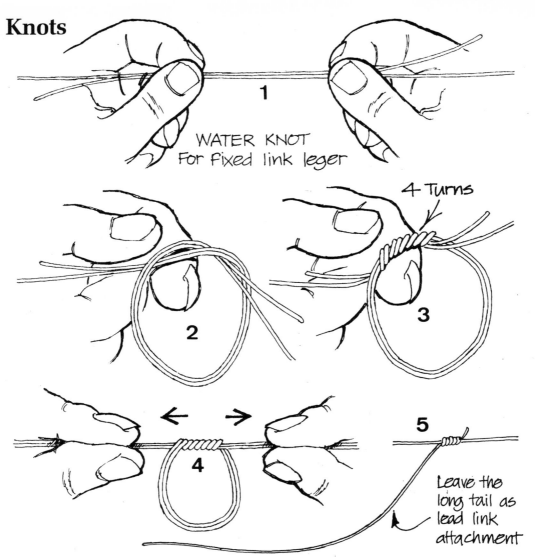

WATER KNOT
For fixed link leger

4 Turns

Leave the long tail as lead link attachment

SLIDING STOP KNOT
For use with sliding float

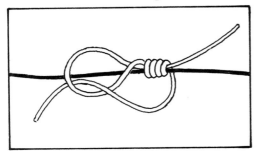

TUCKED HALF-BLOOD KNOT
For eyed hooks and swivels

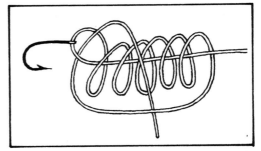

Undertow deposits silt which, over the years, forms a bank on which aquatic plants and fauna thrive, providing a feeding area for roach.

Fishing large lakes and reservoirs

In these vast areas of deep, open water roach location can be a problem. Bill Penney would often fish with the wind in his face at Lambeth Reservoir, and this method of approach is nowadays commonly adopted by big-fish anglers, whether they are fishing for roach or carp.

As roach always seem to be more responsive during a period of poor light, mild, overcast weather with a wind of about force 4 will provide the best results.

Casting a float rig should present no problems, provided it is suitably weighted, such as the float leger. If the wind does interfere then a change to a leger rig may be the solution.

The introduction of half a dozen balls of brown or white crumb stuffed with maggots and casters should be made via a groundbait catapult or by hand. Accuracy is vital and the use of a marker buoy will ensure that this is attained.

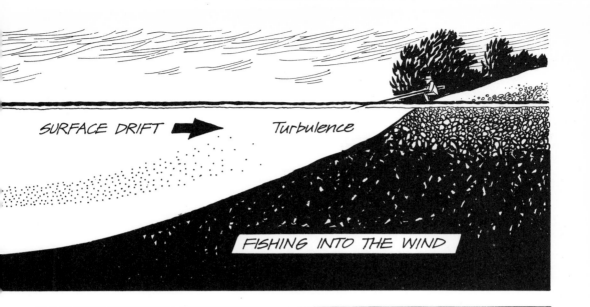

SURFACE DRIFT ➡ Turbulence

FISHING INTO THE WIND

MARKER BUOY (Large sliding float)

Loop Loop

Bead ← Soluble PVA strip

The marker buoy is cast just beyond the feeding area, where the PVA will dissolve. The buoy can be retrieved by snagging it with a treble hook.
(Marker buoy as featured in Jim Gibbinson's book, 'Modern Specimen Hunting'.)

1½oz (40g) lead

Feeding Area

The roach found in these venues are usually large, travelling around in groups rather than big shoals.

Bites may not be frequent but the rewards can more than compensate the patient angler. Baits, therefore, need to be readily visible — the presence of silkweed on the bottom may smother a bait such as maggot, but more buoyant material such as bread flake or crust can be used.

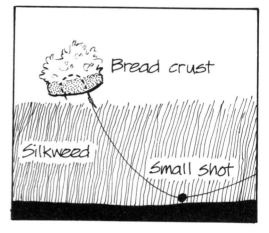

The presence of silkweed can be ascertained by dragging a plummet and treble hook through the area.

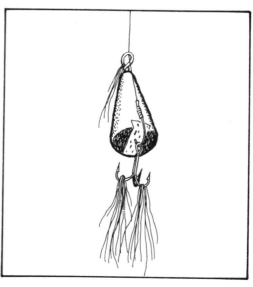

Groundbaiting

Catapults

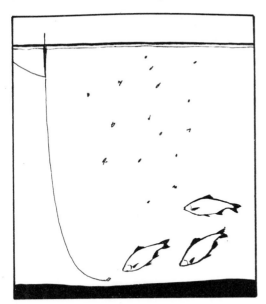

Loose feed when roach are active

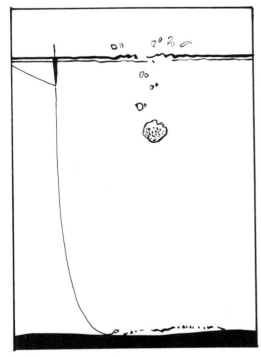

Groundbait during quiet spells

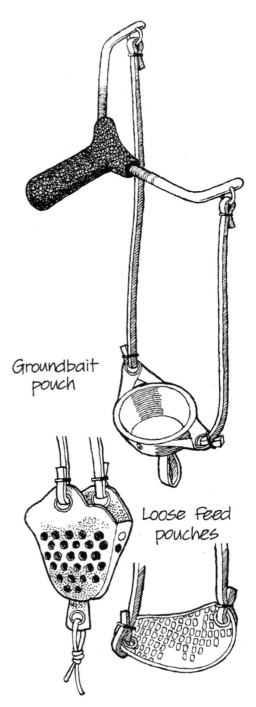

Groundbait
pouch

Loose feed
pouches

Leger tackle for roach

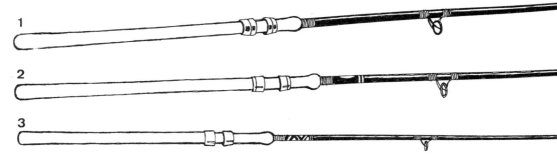

RODS

① 9 or 10ft (2·75 or 3·05m) leger rod with threaded tip ring to accommodate a swingtip or a screw-in quivertip.

② 10 or 11 ft (3·05 or 3·35m) feeder rod.

③ 6 or 7 ft (1·85 or 2·15m) wand with alternative tips.

ACCESSORIES

④ Screw-in quiver/springtip
⑤ Screw-in swingtip
⑥ Swivel
⑦ Link swivel
⑧ Leger stop
⑨ Leger link bead
⑩ Selection of casting bombs ¼–1oz (7–30g)
⑪ Open-end feeder
⑫ Block-end feeder
⑬ Drennan block-end feeder
⑭ Butt indicator
⑮ Non-toxic split shot
⑯ Selection of spade-end and eyed hooks, sizes 18–10 stored in hook wallet.

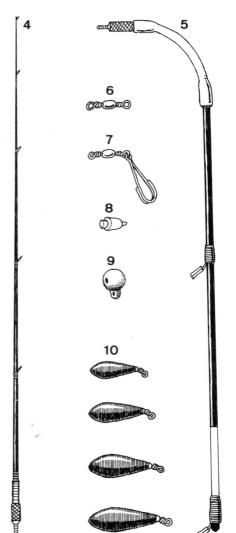

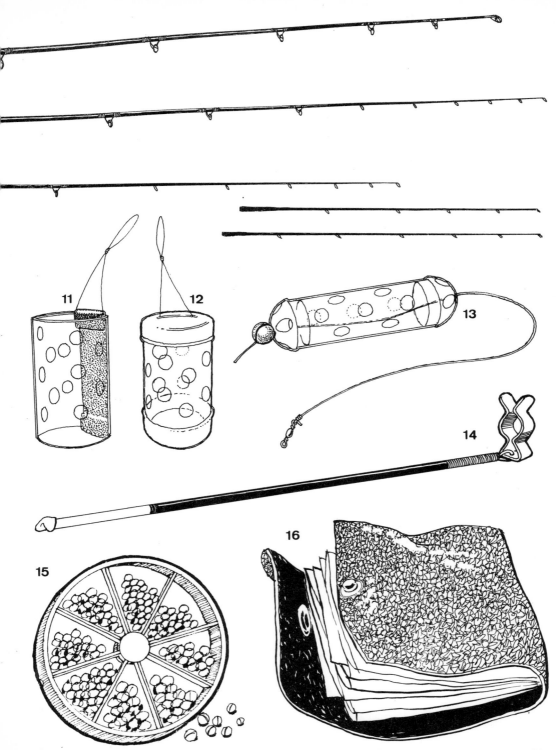

11

12

13

14

15

16

Terminal leger rigs

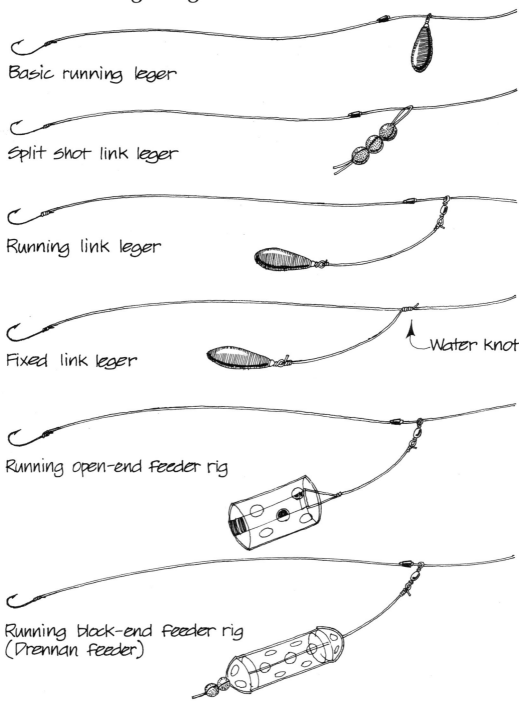

Basic running leger

Split shot link leger

Running link leger

Fixed link leger

Water knot

Running open-end feeder rig

Running block-end feeder rig
(Drennan feeder)

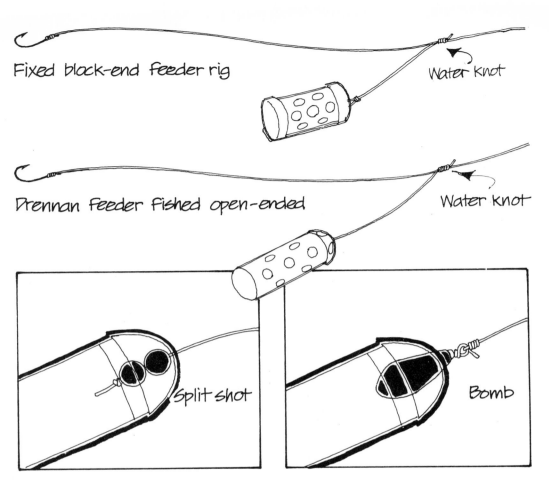

Fixed block-end feeder rig

Water knot

Drennan feeder fished open-ended

Water knot

Split shot

Bomb

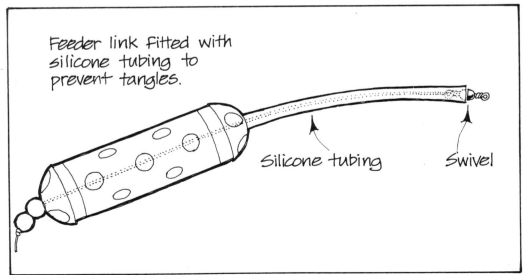

Feeder link fitted with
silicone tubing to
prevent tangles.

Silicone tubing

Swivel

Quick release link system

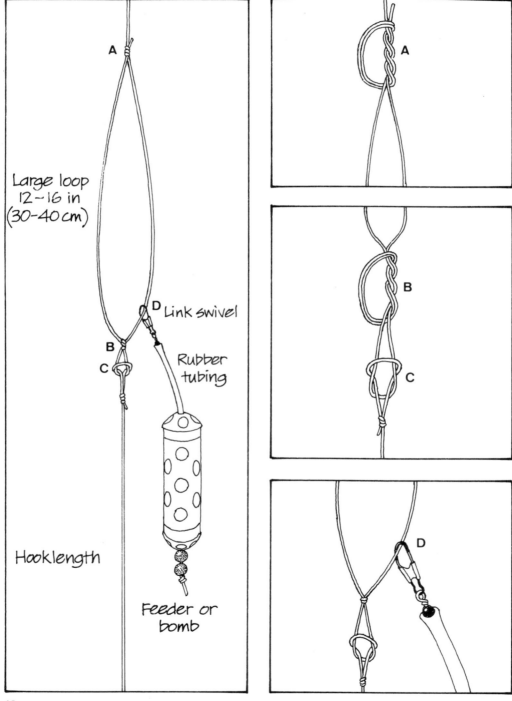

Large loop
12 – 16 in
(30-40 cm)

A

B
C

D Link swivel

Rubber
tubing

Hooklength

Feeder or
bomb

A

B

C

D

Landing net

Keep net

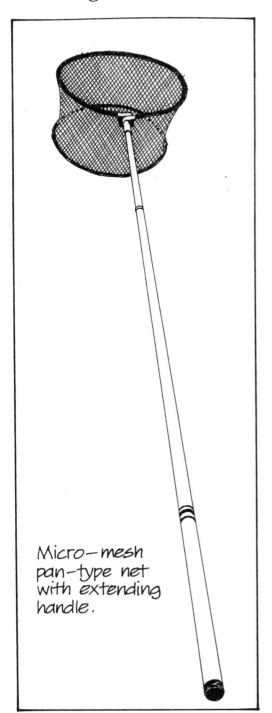

Micro—mesh
pan-type net
with extending
handle.

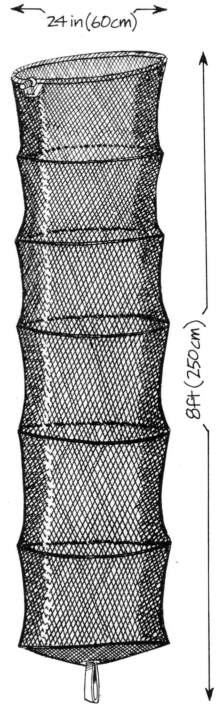

24 in (60 cm)

8 ft (250 cm)

Legering in stillwater

When weather conditions or distance prohibit the use of float tackle, legering is the method which can provide the angler with an opportunity of contacting the larger roach in stillwater. Some specimen hunters use this method exclusively in their quest for jumbo-sized roach.

A 9 or 10ft (2.75 or 3.05m) leger rod will be suitable, combined with a fixed-spool reel loaded with 3lb (1.35kg) line, and a hooklength of 2lb (0.90kg) or 2½lb (1.15kg).

POPULAR BITE INDICATORS FOR STILLWATER ROACH

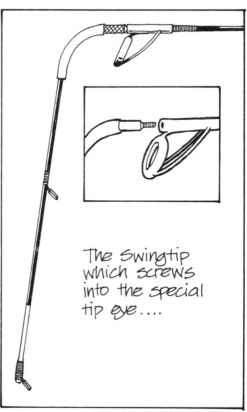

The swingtip which screws into the special tip eye....

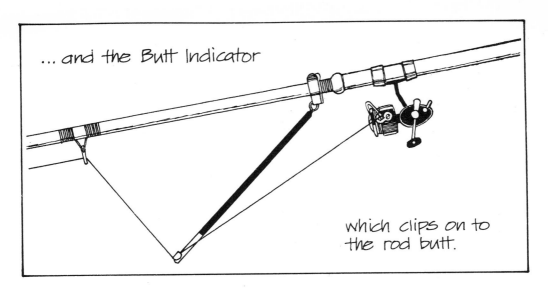

... and the Butt Indicator

which clips on to the rod butt.

Rod rests for legering need to be the type that permit free passage of line ....

...and preferably extendable.

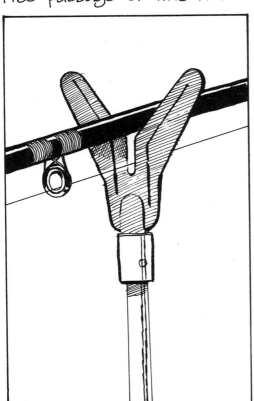

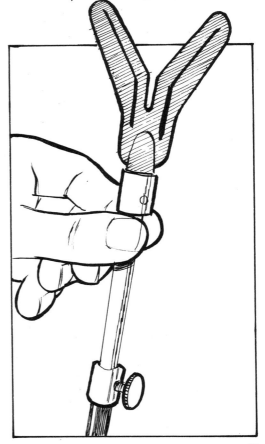

Fishing with a swingtip

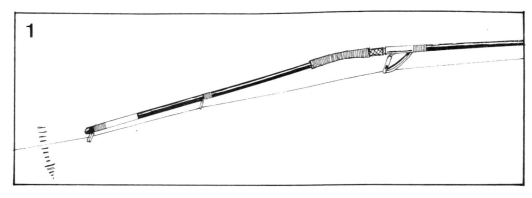

After the cast the rod is placed in the rests. The tip will be in this position as the terminal tackle sinks to the bottom.

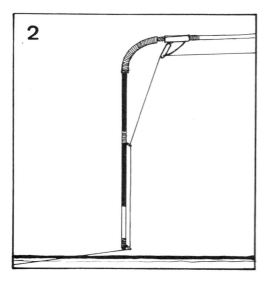

When the terminal tackle has settled, the tip will drop back to hang vertically beneath the rod tip. The rests should be positioned so that the tip is just clear of the water surface.

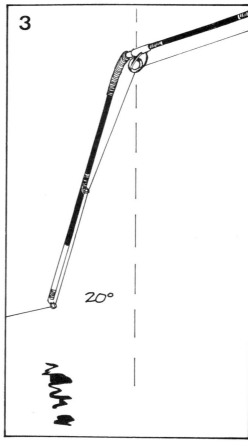

20°

The line is then tightened so that the tip adopts an angle of about 20° off vertical.

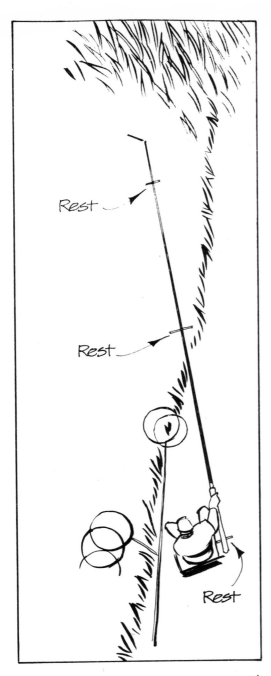

Rest

Rest

Rest

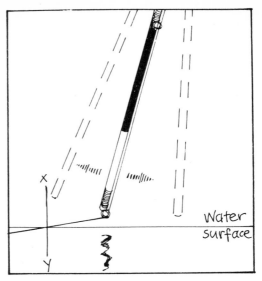

X

Y

Water surface

Bites will register as lifts or drop backs.

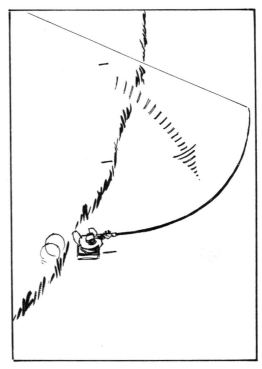

Swingtipping demands 100% concentration. Landing net, keep net, bait and rod butt should be immediately to hand.

Strike by using a long, low sideways sweep of the rod.

Fishing with a butt indicator

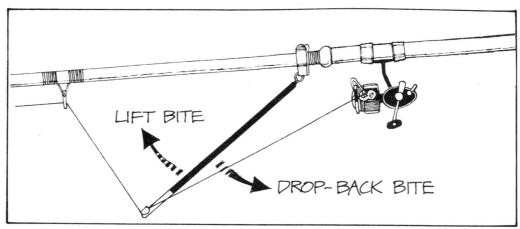

LIFT BITE

DROP-BACK BITE

After the cast has been made and the terminal tackle has sunk to the bottom, the line should be tightened so that the indicator adopts the attitude shown above. Bites will register as lift or drop-back bites.

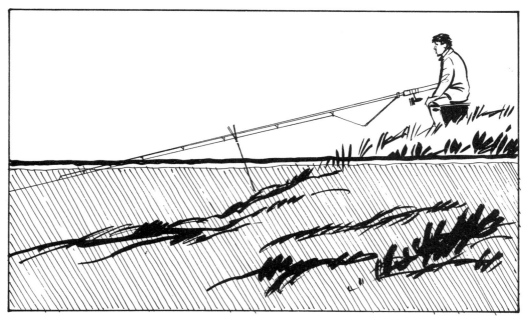

It is always advisable to sink the rod tip below the water surface, especially if wind or surface drift occurs.

Like swingtipping, this method requires maximum concentration, with the rod butt resting immediately to hand.

In ideal conditions, with little or no cross wind, the rod should be pointing directly in line with the bait.

With the wind coming from one side the indicator will need to be shielded in order to prevent buffeting. The rod will probably have to be positioned at a slight angle to the line in order to do this.

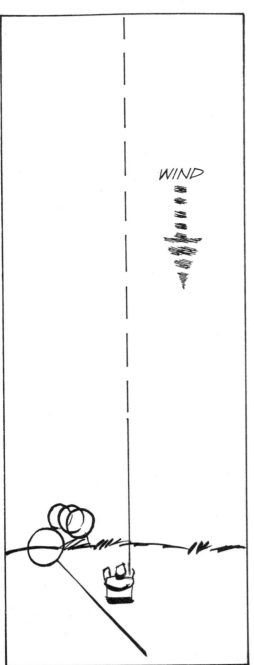

WIND

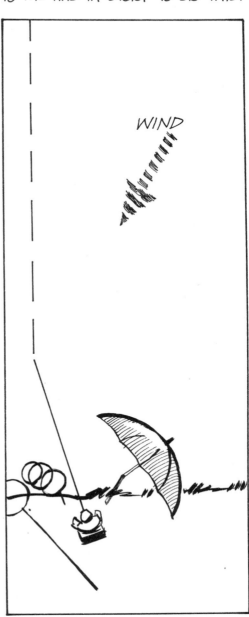

WIND

Float fishing for river roach

Trotting the stream is an ideal method for taking roach on faster flowing rivers.

Line is allowed to flow from the reel at the same speed as the current, presenting the bait to the fish in as natural a manner as possible.

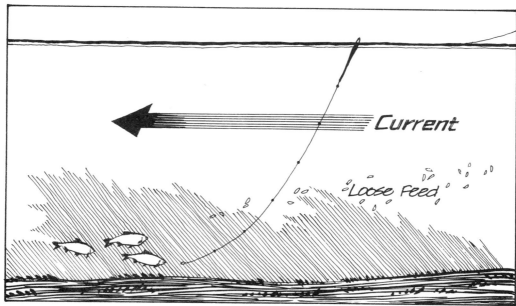

Current

Loose feed

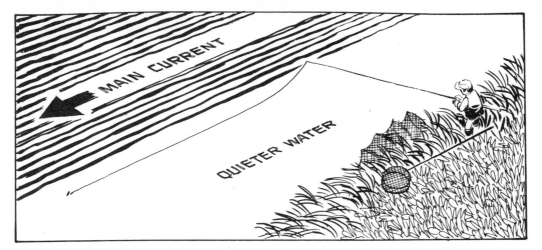

The edge of the main current is often the most productive area, and if this lies one rod length out from the bank so much the better, for this will permit maximum control over the line and terminal tackle.

A fixed-spool, closed-face or centre-pin reel can be used for trotting — the following sequence shows how to pay out line as the float and terminal tackle progresses down-stream.

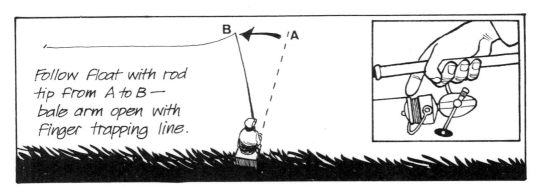

Follow float with rod tip from A to B — bale arm open with finger trapping line.

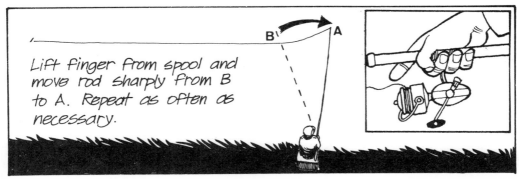

Lift finger from spool and move rod sharply from B to A. Repeat as often as necessary.

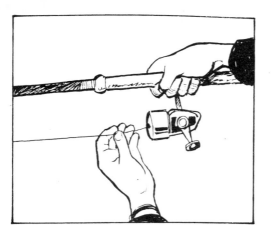

TROTTING WITH A CLOSED FACE REEL

Line does not spill from this reel so freely as it does from an open-faced reel. This makes the closed-face reel popular with many anglers for this form of fishing. Some control with the free hand may be necessary occasionally.

TROTTING WITH A CENTRE-PIN REEL

Just a light pressure on the revolving drum is all that is required.

If the line of the trot is beyond the rod tip the current may produce a belly in the line, dragging the float and bait unnaturally off course. This problem can be rectified by a manoeuvre known as 'mending the line!'

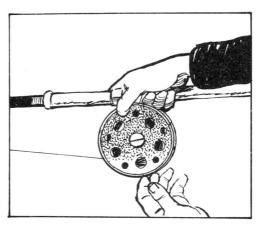

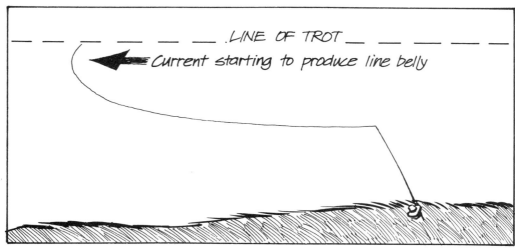

LINE OF TROT

Current starting to produce line belly

Mending the line

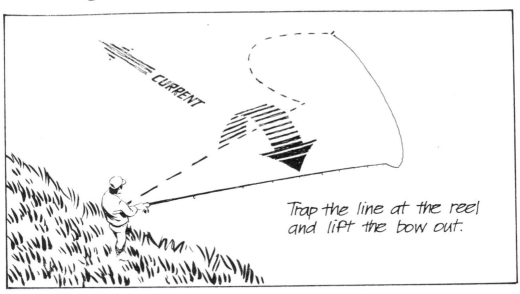

Trap the line at the reel and lift the bow out.

Floats for trotting

Left to right:
STICK
WIRE STEM STICK
AVON
BALSA

Trotting floats are attached top and bottom by float rubber.

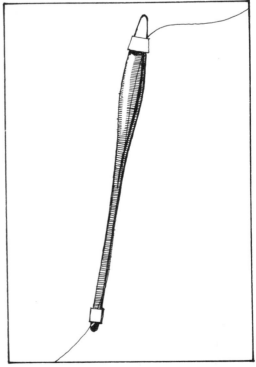

Where to locate roach in fast rivers

Roach tend to avoid the main thrust of the current and shoal up in the slacker and more sheltered areas of the river.

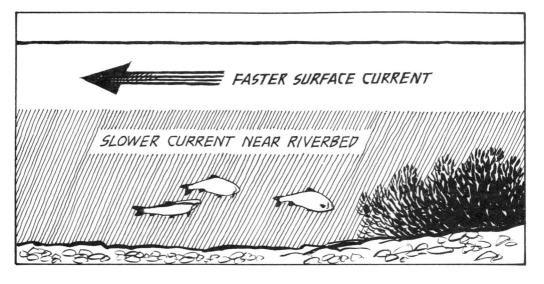

FASTER SURFACE CURRENT

SLOWER CURRENT NEAR RIVERBED

Bed of river shallows off at tail of pool

Trotting rigs

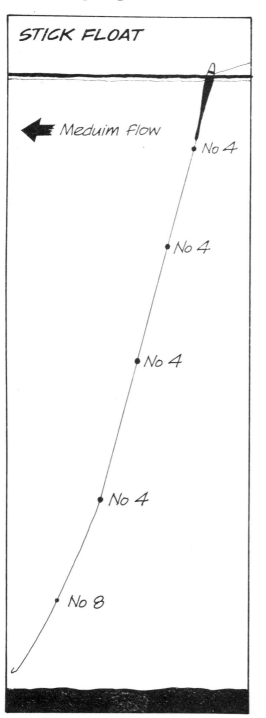

STICK FLOAT

Meduim flow

No 4

No 4

No 4

No 4

No 8

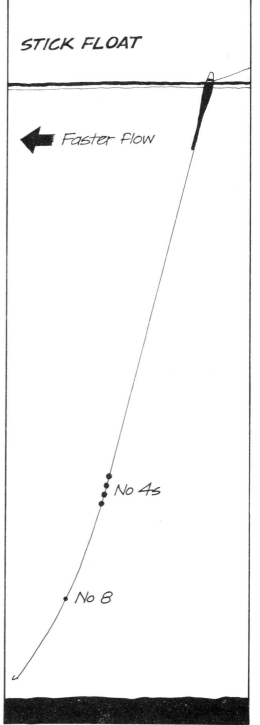

STICK FLOAT

Faster flow

No 4s

No 8

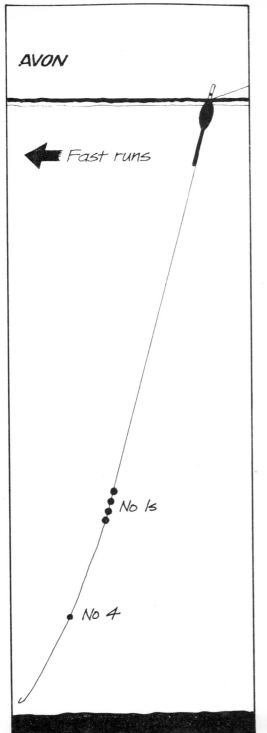

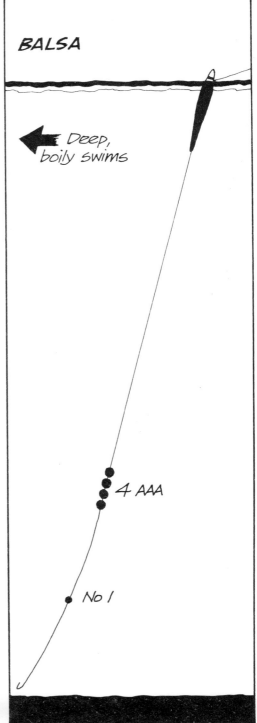

Groundbaiting running water

Water with a steady flow or not too much depth can be fed with helpings of loose maggots, either by hand or catapult.

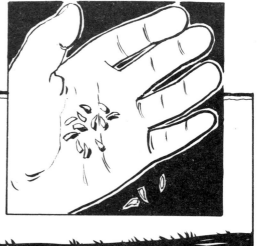

Deeper water with a stronger current will sweep loose-fed maggots too far down-stream unless they are laced into a ball of breadcrumb.

Make a depression in the ball, fill it with maggots and squeeze into a complete ball.

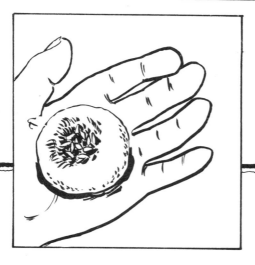

Groundbait balls disintegrate on bottom, releasing maggots into fishing area.

The baitdropper is a very useful gadget for depositing loose maggots at close range on the bottom, in areas of deep, fast water.

Method of attachment

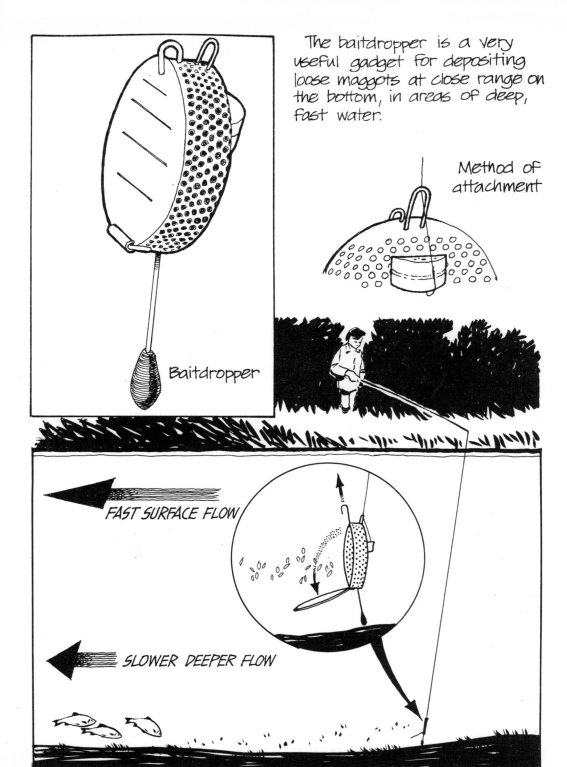

Baitdropper

FAST SURFACE FLOW

SLOWER DEEPER FLOW

the ideal situation when trotting a float through a swim is to present the hookbait amidst the items of loose feed. Loose feed should be used sparingly as overlarge helpings may have the effect of making the roach fall back downstream, out of range of the trotting area.

Small maggots, pinkies and squatts, are best for loose feed and groundbait. These can be kept in a separate container from the large white hookbait maggots.

A brand of monofilament line which has a tendency to float is most suitable for this form of fishing as it permits a quick, clean lift-off on the strike. The top float rubber should be positioned so that it lies just beneath the surface.

Pinkies Squatts

Large whites

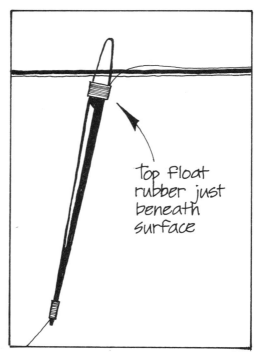

top float rubber just beneath surface

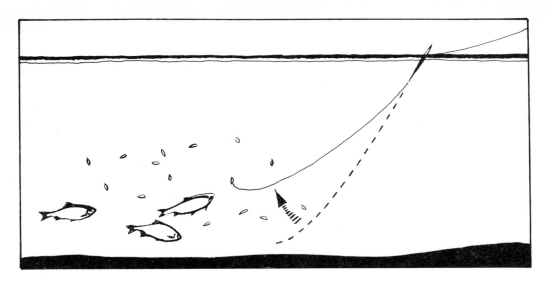

Holding back a trotted float can often induce a bite, as the bait will rise up in the water in a very enticing manner.

ROACH BITES

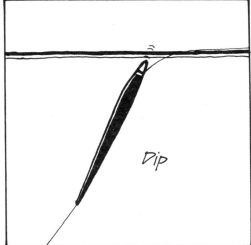

Dip

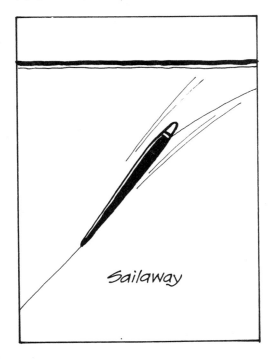

Sailaway

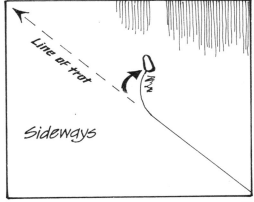

Line of trot

Sideways

IDEAL TROTTING
SITUATION

FLOW

LINE OF TROT

LINE OF RETRIEVE

Roach

LIGHT WIND

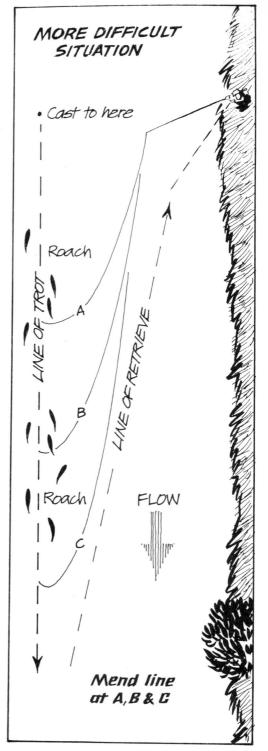

MORE DIFFICULT
SITUATION

• Cast to here

Roach

A

LINE OF TROT

B

LINE OF RETRIEVE

Roach

FLOW

C

Mend line
at A, B & C

An upstream wind can be useful for holding back.

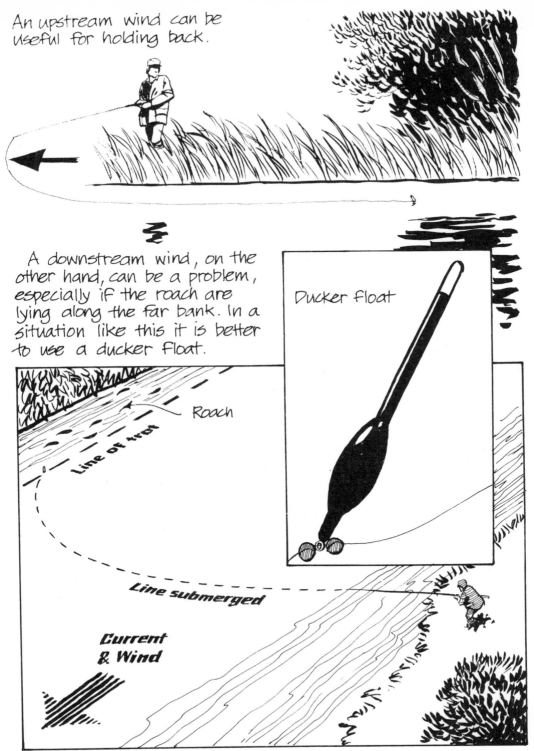

A downstream wind, on the other hand, can be a problem, especially if the roach are lying along the far bank. In a situation like this it is better to use a ducker float.

Ducker float

Roach

Line of trot

Line submerged

Current & Wind

There will be times, when trotting a float, when it is advantageous to set up a fishing position in the river, provided that it is safe to do so. A bait apron is useful here, having an ample bait pouch. The landing net can be placed on two rod rests and the keep net can be anchored on the river bed.

Gardner dual purpose 'Angle-loc'!

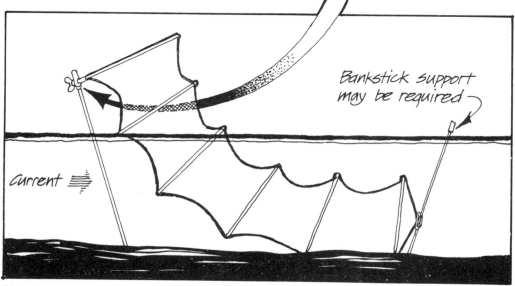

Bankstick support may be required

Current

Stret pegging

A method ideally suited to searching out swims of moderate depth and flow which lie close to the bank. Bankside cover such as reeds is an advantage for this relatively close-range fishing.

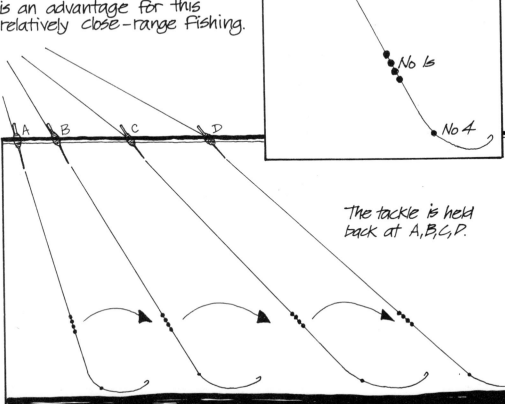

Avon or balsa float

No 1s

No 4

The tackle is held back at A, B, C, D.

Laying on

This is a useful method to employ in the slacker areas of a high-running river during the winter.

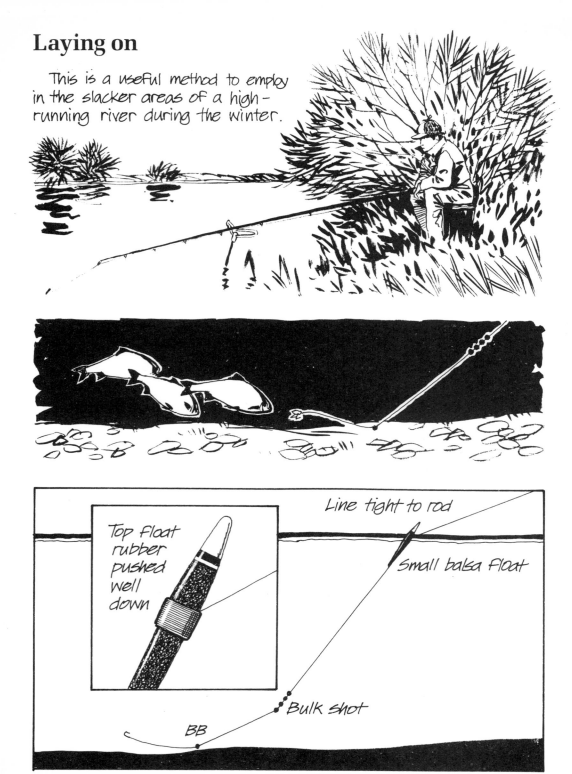

Top float rubber pushed well down

Line tight to rod

Small balsa float

Bulk shot

BB

The quality of roach fishing often improves on rivers during winter, whereas the opposite is often the case on many stillwaters. Laying on is the ideal method for taking advantage of features which become more pronounced with the introduction of winter's extra water supply. The two examples below are typical laying on situations.

MAIN CURRENT

EDDY

FLOODED AREA

MAIN CURRENT

Float fishing on sluggish rivers

Waggler tactics are ideally suited to sluggish rivers, especially the wider ones. With the line sunk beneath the surface down-stream wind problems can be overcome.

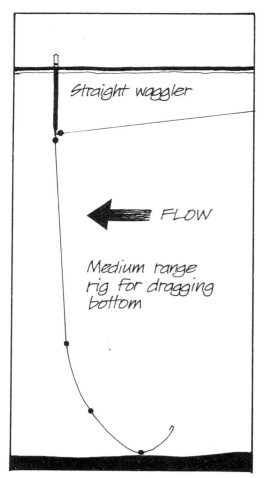

Straight waggler

FLOW

Medium range rig for dragging bottom

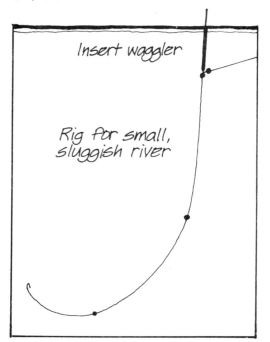

Insert waggler

Rig for small, sluggish river

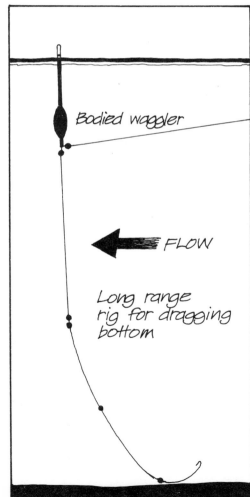

Bodied waggler

FLOW

Long range rig for dragging bottom

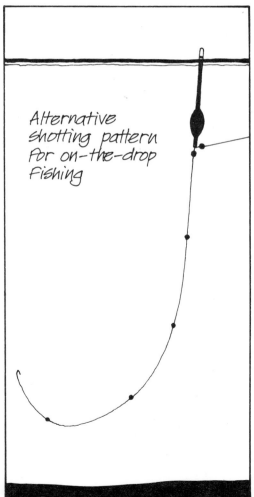

Alternative shotting pattern for on-the-drop fishing

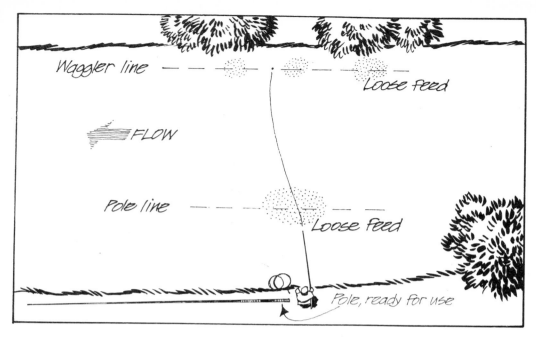

A two line approach will often keep the roach angler in contact with feeding fish, when fishing on very slow-running rivers and canals. Loose feed is introduced at regular intervals to both lines of attack. If one line ceases to produce fish, the other line will be there, ready baited.

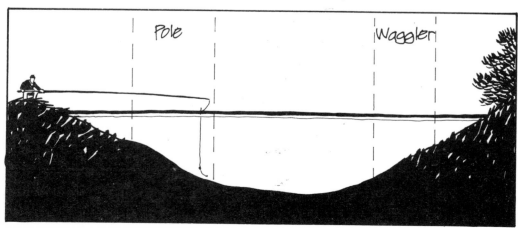

Legering for river roach

Legering with a feeder rig is now probably the most widely practised form of legering on the larger rivers. The angler using this method can feel confident that the hookbait and feed are being presented in precisely the same area.

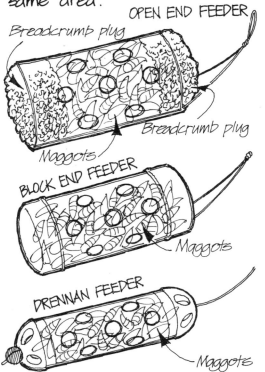

OPEN END FEEDER

Breadcrumb plug

Breadcrumb plug

Maggots

BLOCK END FEEDER

Maggots

DRENNAN FEEDER

Maggots

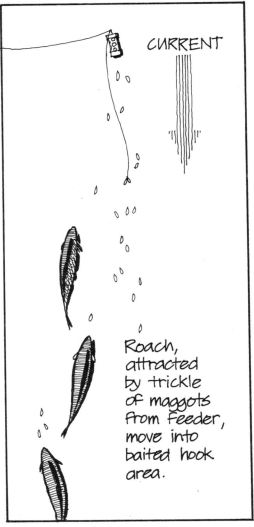

CURRENT

Roach, attracted by trickle of maggots from feeder, move into baited hook area.

Casting a swimfeeder should be done with a smooth, easy action. The feeder should hang motionless at point A and be aimed at a point above the target area. Lining up with a feature on the far bank, such as a bush or tree, will guarantee consistently accurate casts.

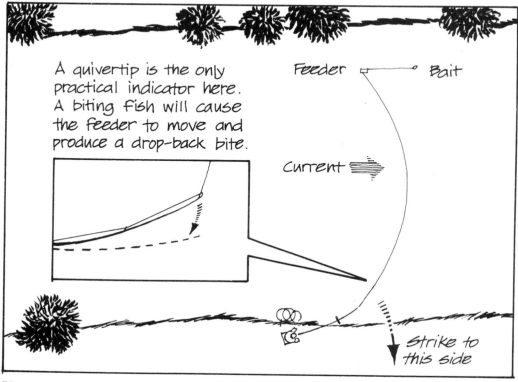

A quivertip is the only practical indicator here. A biting fish will cause the feeder to move and produce a drop-back bite.

Feeder

Bait

Current

Strike to this side

If the current causes the feeder to trundle along the riverbed, the rod can be rested at a high angle. With less line under the surface the pressure is reduced and the problem overcome.

Legering on smaller rivers is best done with a smaller leger rod, minus the feeder which may cause too much disturbance in confined spaces. A shot link leger is far more suitable. A mobile approach is often more productive, fishing for a while and moving on if there is no response or if a swim ceases to produce fish.

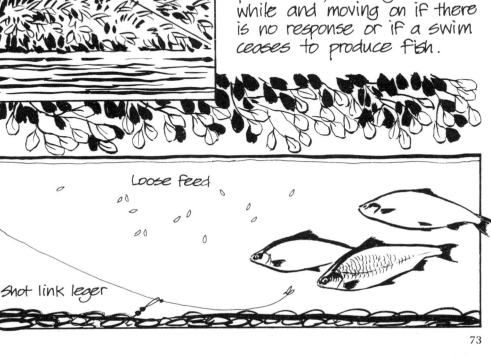

Loose feed

Shot link leger

Canal roach

TOW PATH

NEARSIDE SHELF

Start by fishing cloud groundbait and bread-punch hookbait....

... later, switch to hempseed further down the shelf.

BOAT CHANNEL
This area is usually unfishable unless boat traffic is very light, or during winter.

This bait will receive instant attention from the smaller roach which are often located on the top of the nearside shelf. A breadpunch tool will be required to cut the sliced bread into neat, little hook-sized pieces.

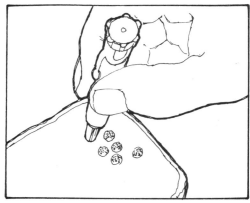

BREADPUNCH
with spare tips

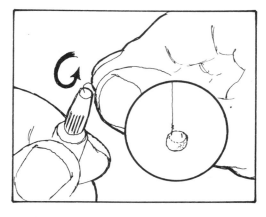

Loosefeed maggots via catapult from time-to-time as fish may be spooked from nearside shelf in clear water.

FAR SHELF

Always a good roach area, especially with overhanging foliage (eg., elderberry). Use a long pole or rod and waggler rig.

Legering on canals

Should windy weather make float presentation impossible, leger tactics will often prove very effective. A 6 or 7 ft (1·85 or 2·15 m) wand, used quivertip style, is easy to tuck behind the shelter of a fishing umbrella. A shot link leger will provide the end rig as long casts will not be necessary.

Pole fishing

The pole is ideally suited to catching fast-biting roach and is favoured by many top match anglers, especially on the continent.

Flick tip with eye

Flick tip with D.A.M. Quicktip attachment

Hollow top section with elastic shock absorber

A flick tip is used for smaller finicky roach, as it has a more immediate striking action.

The elastic shock absorber set-up will cope with larger fish. The drawing below shows the shock absorber in action.

Pole floats come in a vast array of shapes and sizes, but most are attached to the line in the same manner.

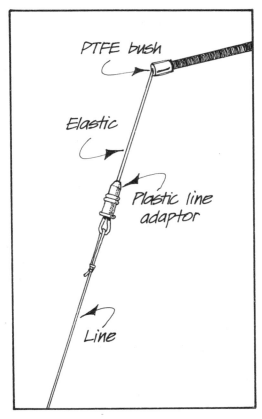

PTFE bush

Elastic

Plastic line adaptor

Line

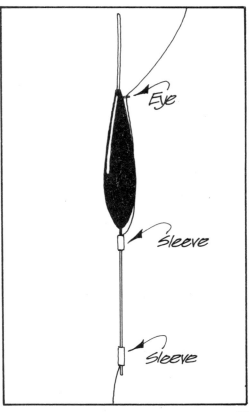

Eye

Sleeve

Sleeve

The most comfortable way of holding a fully extended pole while waiting for a bite is to rest it across the knees.

When a fish is hooked, sections of the pole must be unshipped to make landing the fish possible.

Pole roller makes this operation easier

On the other hand, when fishing close in, using the top 2 or 3 metres of the pole, there will be no need to dismantle at all. The smaller roach usually found here can be swung to hand.

Pole terminal rigs for canals

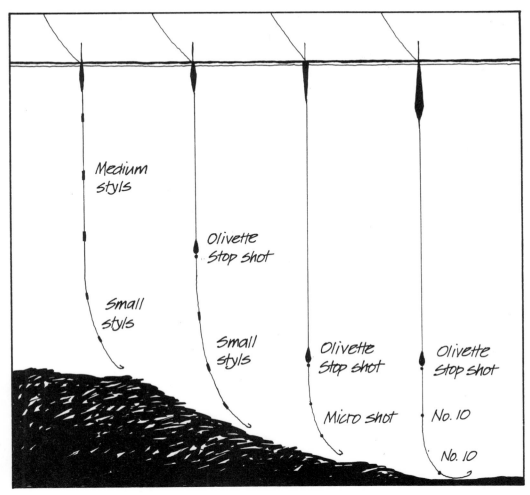

Medium styls

Small styls

Olivette Stop shot

Small styls

Olivette Stop shot

Micro shot

Olivette Stop shot

No. 10

No. 10

Pole rigs should be made up at home and wound on to pole winders, ready for instant use at the waterside.

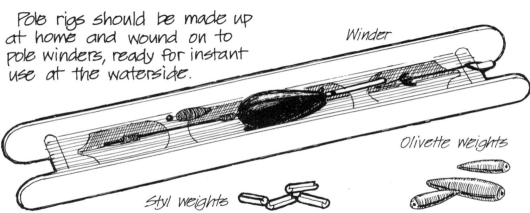

Winder

Olivette weights

Styl weights